AIR FORCE

Simon Rose

www.av2books.com

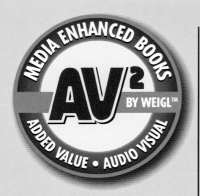

AV² provides enriched content that supplements and complements this book. Weigl's AV² books strive to create inspired learning and engage young minds in a total learning experience.

Your AV² Media Enhanced books come alive with...

Audio
Listen to sections of the book read aloud.

Key Words
Study vocabulary, and complete a matching word activity.

Video
Watch informative video clips.

Quizzes
Test your knowledge.

Embedded Weblinks
Gain additional information for research.

Slide Show
View images and captions, and prepare a presentation.

Try This!
Complete activities and hands-on experiments.

... and much, much more!

Go to www.av2books.com, and enter this book's unique code.

BOOK CODE

P 2 7 5 8 1 9

AV² by Weigl brings you media enhanced books that support active learning.

Published by AV² by Weigl
350 5th Avenue, 59th Floor
New York, NY 10118
Website: www.av2books.com www.weigl.com

Library of Congress Cataloging-in-Publication Data
Rose, Simon.
  Air Force / Simon Rose.
     p. cm. -- (U.S. Armed Forces)
 Includes index.
 Audience: Grades 4-6.
ISBN 978-1-61913-292-4 (hbk. : alk. paper) -- ISBN 978-1-61913-295-5 (pbk. : alk. paper)
1. United States. Air Force--Juvenile literature. I. Title.
 UG633.R67 2012
 358.400973--dc23   2012020690

Printed in the United States of America in North Mankato, Minnesota
1 2 3 4 5 6 7 8 9 16 15 14 13 12

062012
WEP170512

Project Coordinator: Aaron Carr
Design: Mandy Christiansen

Every reasonable effort has been made to trace ownership and to obtain permission to reprint copyright material. The publisher would be pleased to have any errors or omissions brought to their attention so that they may be corrected in subsequent printings.

Weigl acknowledges Getty Images as its primary image supplier for this title.

CONTENTS

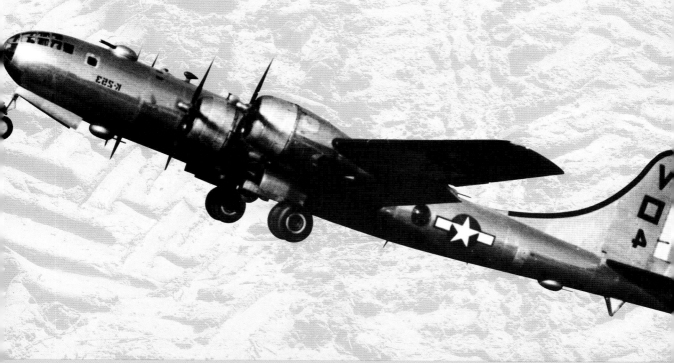

WHAT IS THE AIR FORCE?

The Air Force is one of the main branches of the United States Armed Forces. The other branches are the Army, the Navy, the Marine Corps, and the Coast Guard. The Air Force is the aviation and air warfare force of the United States military. This means it is made up of forces that operate planes and weapons that attack the enemy from the sky. The Air Force is the newest branch of the Armed Forces. It was founded in 1947.

The Air Force is part of the Department of Defense. This department is in charge of all five branches of the military. The secretary of defense is the head of this department. The president of the United States is commander-in-chief of the entire Armed Forces. The U.S. Air Force is the largest air force in the world. It has more than 300,000 people on full-time active duty and about 175,000 personnel in the **Air National Guard** and **Air Force Reserve**. Both men and women in the Air Force are known as airmen.

★ Air Force pilots are trained to fly dangerous missions over enemy territory.

STRUCTURE OF THE U.S. ARMED FORCES

| Marine Corps | Army | Air Force | Navy | Coast Guard |

| Combat controllers | Pararescuemen |

PROTECTING THE COUNTRY

The U.S. Air Force defends the United States and protects its interests around the world. The Air Force leads U.S. military attacks in and from the air. The Air Force supports the Army, Navy, and Marines in combat missions on land and water. It does this by using fighter jets, bombers, missiles, and cargo transport aircraft, and **surveillance** information from **unmanned aircraft** and space satellites. The Air Force is also responsible for keeping the United States safe from enemy attacks from the air.

The U.S. Air National Guard and the Air Force Reserve support the Air Force. Each state has its own Air National Guard. The Air National Guard can be called upon to provide personnel and equipment when needed. The federal government is in charge of the Air Force Reserve. The Reserve works with the Air Force on a daily basis in the United States and around the world. However, reservists do not work on active duty as their full-time job.

On the Front Lines

In times of war, the Air Force is in charge of air attacks against enemy military sites, such as fuel stations and weapons factories. It also attacks enemy land forces from the air, often to support U.S. forces already fighting the enemy on the ground. The Air Force leads combat missions against enemy air forces. It also takes part in **reconnaissance** missions. This helps the U.S. military obtain information about enemy activities away from the battlefield.

AIR FORCE CORE VALUES

INTEGRITY FIRST Do what is right even when no one is looking. Have courage, be honest, take responsibility for your actions, and be fair to others.

SERVICE BEFORE SELF Your military duties are more important than your own desires. Follow rules, put the needs of the troops ahead of your own, be confident and optimistic in difficult situations, and have faith in your leaders.

EXCELLENCE IN ALL WE DO Dedicate yourself to improvement and innovation. Take classes that further your education, and stay in good physical and mental shape. When working with others to reach a common goal, show them respect and do not judge them. This will help get the job done with the best possible results.

HISTORY OF THE AIR FORCE

The Air Force became a separate branch of the U.S. Armed Forces in 1947. Before then, responsibility for aviation operations in the U.S. military was split between the Navy and the Army. The Navy was in charge of operations from aircraft carriers and ships with **amphibious** aircraft, such as helicopters. The Army was responsible for land-based operations. These responsibilities were combined under the Air Force.

1917
★ The U.S. enters World War I

1944
★ D-Day, the Allied invasion of Western Europe, occurs on June 6

1947
★ The U.S. Air Force is officially created

1907
★ Army establishes Aeronautical Division, Signal Corps to oversee aviation operations

1926
★ The Air Service is renamed as the U.S. Air Army Corps

1945
★ Atomic bombs dropped on Hiroshima and Nagasaki, and World War II ends

1914
★ Aviation Section, Signal Corps replaces Aeronautical Division

1918
★ The Air Service, US Army is formed and takes charge of aviation operations in the war, and World War I ends

1941
★ The U.S. Army Air Forces is created as a combat branch of the Army, and the U.S. enters World War II after the Japanese attack on Pearl Harbor

1917

1941

Since it was founded, the Air Force has played a role in every armed conflict the U.S. has been involved in. It sometimes is the first branch of the Armed Forces to launch an attack. In 2003, the Air Force led the U.S. invasion of Iraq in 2003 with heavy bombing and missile strikes on Baghdad. This made it easier for U.S. ground forces to attack the city.

BERLIN AIRLIFT

The year after it was officially founded, the Air Force faced its first major test. In 1948, the Soviet Union blocked road and air traffic into Berlin, the capital of Germany. From June 26, 1948, to September 30, 1949, the U.S. Air Force and Britain's Royal Air Force flew supplies into the city, saving Berlin's people from starvation. It also ended the Soviet blockade. This operation became known as the Berlin Airlift.

1950 TO 1953
★ Korean War

1990s
★ Air Force involved in NATO operations in Yugoslavia

1989
★ Invasion of Panama

2011
★ Air Force involved in NATO operations in Libya

1965 TO 1973
★ Vietnam War

1983
★ Invasion of Grenada

2003
★ Invasion of Iraq

2001
★ Invasion of Afghanistan

1965

2003

THE AIR FORCE AROUND THE WORLD

In addition to its bases on the United States mainland, the Air Force also operates bases in Hawaii and Alaska, and in many different countries around the world. It also shares some bases with armed forces of other countries.

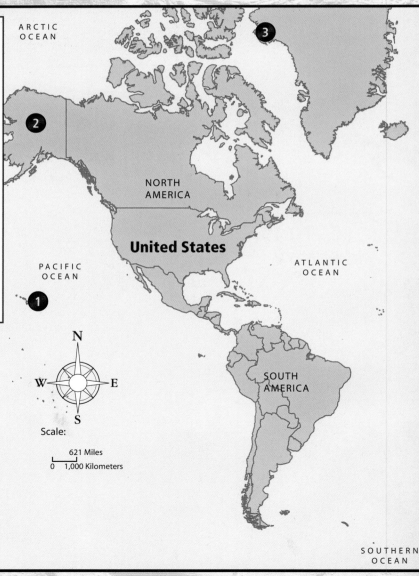

❶ Hawai'i

Pacific Air Forces is headquartered at Hickham Air Force Base in Hawai'i. This Air Force command is in charge of aviation operations of the U.S. military in the Pacific Ocean region. It has nine Air Force bases and almost 400 aircraft under its command. Its area of responsibility stretches from the North Pole to the South Pole and from the west coast of the United States to the east coast of Africa. This area is home to more than half of the world's population and 36 nations.

❷ Alaska

Clear Air Force Station is an early warning site in central Alaska. This means it is responsible for detecting long-range enemy missiles launched at the United States. It uses high-technology radar systems to do this. The station also provides surveillance data from space satellites to Air Force Space Command in Colorado.

Greenland

Thule Air Base is further north than any other U.S. military site. It is 947 miles (1,524 km) from the North Pole. The base has about 600 personnel. It is home to the 12th Space Warning Squadron, which has responsibility for detecting long-range missiles heading toward the United States. These missiles are called intercontinental ballistic missiles, or ICBMs for short.

3

Germany

Ramstein Air Base is the headquarters of United States Air Forces in Europe, which is responsible for all Air Force operations in Europe. Ramstein is also a North Atlantic Treaty Organization (NATO) facility. Personnel at the base come from almost every country in Europe.

4

Qatar

Al Udeid Air Base is located in Doha on the Persian Gulf. It is home to the Air Force Central Command. The command is part of the U.S. Central Command, which also is based at Al Udeid. The U.S. Central Command is in charge of all Armed Forces operations in the Middle East, Central Asia, and East Africa.

5

ARCTIC
OCEAN

ASIA

6 4

EUROPE

5

AFRICA

INDIAN
OCEAN

PACIFIC
OCEAN

United Kingdom

6

The U.S. Air Force operates a number of facilities at Royal Air Force (RAF) bases of the United Kingdom. RAF Mildenhall is a refueling stop for Air Force planes flying between the United States and Europe or the Middle East. The refueling can be done either at the airfield or by hooking up to a refueling plane in mid-air. The Air Force also has forces at RAF Molesworth and RAF Alconbury. Both of these bases played a major role in operations against Germany in World War II.

AIR FORCE UNIFORMS

U.S. airmen have worn a number of different uniforms through the years. For pilots of early military aircraft, the most important need was for clothing to be warm. The pilots sat in an unheated **cockpit** that had no roof. It could be freezing cold because of the wind from the propeller and the lower temperatures high in the sky. Combat planes with heated, enclosed cockpits were not used until late in World War II.

WORLD WAR I

The Sidcot suit was similar to overalls. It was made from leather and had a fur lining. The cuffs were also lined with fur to prevent warm air from escaping. A fur collar could be attached to the suit. In addition to keeping pilots warm, the suit protected the pilot from oil flung out from the engines.

Pilots wore a leather cap with earflaps. They also used goggles and gloves.

WORLD WAR II

Airmen in combat planes wore jackets made of leather, often with fur collars. Shearling jackets were the warmest type of flight jackets. They were made from sheepskin, lined with fur or wool.

Airmen who operated **gun turrets** had to fire through open windows. They wore electrically heated flight suits to stay warm. They also wore vests known as flak jackets to protect themselves from flying **shrapnel** from anti-aircraft guns. These vests had steel plates sewn into them. Life preservers and parachutes were used in emergencies.

TODAY

Pilots have a parachute and a life preserver to use in emergencies. They also use a survival vest that contains emergency items. These items include flares, a supply of water, ammunition, knives, medical supplies, and more.

The current Air Force flight suit is made of lightweight, fireproof material called Nomex. The suits are usually green or tan in color and have several large pockets.

The flight helmet has a visor and an oxygen mask.

AIR FORCE AIRCRAFT

WORLD WAR I

The Curtiss JN-4 "Jenny" was used to train military pilots in North America, although it was never used in combat. It was a biplane, which means it had two main wings, one above the other. The plane had a top speed of 75 miles (121 km) per hour and could operate at heights of 6,500 feet (1,980 m).

WORLD WAR II

The P-47 Thunderbolt was one of the main U.S. fighter planes in World War II. The aircraft had eight machine guns and won many battles with enemy fighter planes. The plane was also used as a bomber for ground attacks.

The B-29 Superfortress bomber was one of the largest aircraft used during the war. It also had some of the most advanced technology, including remote-controlled machine-gun turrets. The B-29 was the main aircraft used in American **firebombing** attacks on Japan. It was also used to drop atomic bombs on Hiroshima and Nagasaki in August 1945.

TODAY

The F-16 is the most popular fighter plane in the world. More than 4,400 F-16s have been built for air forces of 25 countries around the world. The U.S. Air Force has more than 1,500 F-16s. The aircraft has a top speed of 1,500 miles (2,400 km) per hour and can fly to a height of 50,000 feet (15,200 m). Its guns can launch a variety of missiles and bombs.

The B-2 Spirit is also known as the Stealth Bomber. It uses special technology to help it avoid detection by enemy radar. The bomber can drop up to 80 500-pound bombs on a single flight.

Air Force One is the plane used to transport the president of the United States. The aircraft has three levels. The lower level is for cargo and the upper level contains the cockpit and the communications room. The middle level has offices, meeting rooms, and living quarters. The plane can carry 26 crew members and up to 70 passengers. It can be refueled while it is in the air and keep flying for long periods if needed.

UNITED STATES OF AMERICA

28000

JOINING THE AIR FORCE

Anyone wishing to join the Air Force must be a U.S. citizen or permanent resident. They must be between 18 and 27 years of age, have a high school education, and be in good physical condition. To qualify for officer programs, a person must have a college degree.

Applying to the Air Force

Step One: Apply on line

Step Two: Talk to a recruiter

Step Three: Take the Armed Forces Vocational Aptitude Battery test (AFVAB)

Step Four: Visit the Military Entrance Processing Station (MEPS), where it is determined if you are qualified to join the Air Force

OATH OF ENLISTMENT

" I do solemnly swear that I will support and defend the Constitution of the United States against all enemies, foreign and domestic; that I will bear true faith and allegiance to the same; and that I will obey the orders of the President of the United States and the orders of the officers appointed over me, according to regulations and the Uniform Code of Military Justice. So help me God. "

Boot Camp Basic Training for Air Force recruits is sometimes called Boot Camp. The training takes place at Lackland Air Force Base near San Antonio, Texas, and is 8-1/2 weeks long. It includes combat and marksmanship training, physical training, and training in first-aid procedures. Following Basic Training, airmen attend technical classes to learn the jobs they will do in the Air Force. Those who wish to become officers may attend the U.S. Air Force Academy in Colorado Springs, Colorado, or Officer Training School at Maxwell Air Force Base in Alabama.

JOBS IN THE AIR FORCE

Being in the Air Force is not just about flying combat missions. There are many types of careers in the Air Force. There are jobs working with computers and technology, fixing and maintaining aircraft, and working in health care or as an engineer. There are also jobs in transportation, arts and education, business, communications, and more. The training and experience gained in the Air Force can lead to successful careers in **civilian** life after military service is completed.

Information and Technology

Jobs in this field involve working in high-tech areas such as computers and communication systems. Air Force **intelligence** specialists study photographs taken from aircraft and satellites to discover information needed by the military. There are also jobs using and repairing electronic systems involved with satellite communications, radar, and navigation.

Business and Administration

Administrative jobs involve keeping accurate information on personnel, equipment, money, and supplies. This is necessary for the Air Force to plan and manage its operations. Administrative personnel may work in a specialized area, such as accounting, finance, business management, legal affairs, and human resources.

Health Care

Air Force doctors and nurses take care of sick or wounded military personnel. They also may provide **humanitarian** health services for civilians in areas hit by earthquakes, floods, or other natural disasters. Careers include working as doctors, nurses, dentists, and physical therapists. Other jobs involve laboratory research or operating medical tools such as x-ray and ultrasound equipment.

Air Force Community Life

In many ways, life in the Air Force is much like civilian life. Airmen work regular hours at a job, they spend time with their families, and they fill their free time with hobbies, sports, or any activity they choose. Some airmen live in barracks, but others live in houses either on or off the base.

Many Air Force bases have all of the facilities of most towns or cities. This may include hospitals, schools, day-care centers, libraries, sports facilities, and shopping malls. The Air Force provides a wide variety of programs to improve the quality of life for families living on Air Force bases. These include counseling services, programs to improve on-base education and job opportunities for family members, and programs that help families deal with the stress of having a parent working in a combat area overseas.

★ Many airmen live with their family on Air Force bases. Some bases are huge and have all the facilities of a town or city.

WRITE YOUR STORY

If you apply to join the Air Force, you will need to write an essay about yourself. This is also true when you apply to a college or for a job. Practice telling your story by completing this writing activity.

1 Brainstorming

Start by making notes about your interests. What are your hobbies? Do you like to read? Are you more interested in computers or power tools? Then, organize your ideas into an outline, with a clear beginning, middle, and end.

2 Writing the First Draft

A first draft does not have to be perfect. Try to get the story written. Then, read it to see if it makes sense. It will probably need revision. Even the most famous writers edit their work many times before it is completed.

3 Editing

Go through your story and remove anything that is repeated or not needed. Also, add any missing information that should be included. Be sure the text makes sense and is easy to read.

4 Proofreading

The proofreading is where you check spelling, grammar, and punctuation. During the proofread, you will often find mistakes that you missed during the editing stage. Always look for ways to make your writing the best it can be.

5 Submitting Your Story

When your text is finished, it is time to submit your story, along with any other application materials. A good essay will increase your chances of being accepted, whether it be for a school, a job, or the Air Force.

TEST YOUR KNOWLEDGE

1 When was the Air Force founded?

2 Where is the headquarters of United States Air Forces in Europe?

3 How many Air Force personnel are on active, full-time duty?

4 What is the most popular fighter jet in the world?

5 Where is the Air Force Academy located?

6 At what age can you apply to join the Air Force?

7 What is the name of the plane that transports the president of the United States?

8 What are the three core values of the U.S. Air Force?

9 Where is Basic Training for Air Force recruits held?

10 What is the most northern U.S. military site?

KEY WORDS

Air Force Reserve: part-time Air Force personnel who can be called to full-time duty in an emergency

Air National Guard: the air forces of individual states that can be called upon when needed

amphibious: operating both on land and on water

civilian: a person who is not an active member of the armed forces

cockpit: the space in a plane where the pilot sits

firebombing: attacking with bombs and missiles to start fires

gun turret: a revolving platform with guns

humanitarian: efforts to save lives and prevent suffering

intelligence: information about the armed forces of another country

reconnaissance: exploration of an area to gain useful information

shrapnel: pieces of metal that fly out of a bullet or bomb when it explodes

surveillance: keeping close watch over an area

unmanned aircraft: a remotely controlled aircraft without a human pilot

INDEX

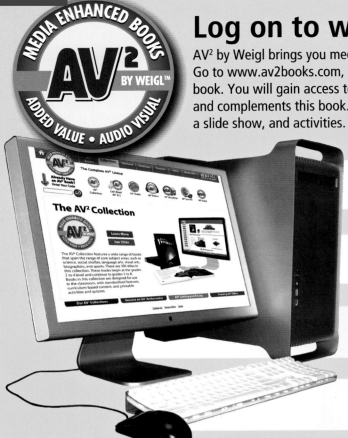

Log on to www.av2books.com

AV² by Weigl brings you media enhanced books that support active learning. Go to www.av2books.com, and enter the special code found on page 2 of this book. You will gain access to enriched and enhanced content that supplements and complements this book. Content includes video, audio, weblinks, quizzes, a slide show, and activities.

Audio
Listen to sections of the book read aloud.

Video
Watch informative video clips.

Embedded Weblinks
Gain additional information for research.

Try This!
Complete activities and hands-on experiments.

WHAT'S ONLINE?

Try This!	Embedded Weblinks	Video	EXTRA FEATURES
Try this timeline activity. Complete a mapping activity. Write an essay about yourself. Test your knowledge of the Air Force.	Read about the importance of the Air Force. Find out more information on the history of the uniform. Learn more about jobs in the Air Force. Read more information about the Air Force.	Watch a video about the Air Force. Check out another video about the Air Force.	**Audio** Listen to sections of the book read aloud. **Key Words** Study vocabulary, and complete a matching word activity. **Slide Show** View images and captions and prepare a presentation **Quizzes** Test your knowledge.

AV² was built to bridge the gap between print and digital. We encourage you to tell us what you like and what you want to see in the future.

Sign up to be an AV² Ambassador at www.av2books.com/ambassador.